the *ki* to *Success*

A woman's
inspiring guide
to having it all

Kirin
Singh

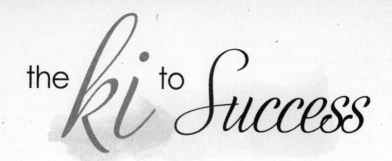

the *ki* to *Success*

A woman's
inspiring guide
to having it all

BURMAN BOOKS
MEDIA CORP.

Published by BurmanBooks Media Corp.
260 Queens Quay West
Suite 1102
Toronto, Ontario
Canada M5J 2N3

Cover design: Diane Kolar
Interior design: Tracey Ogus
Editing: Anna Watson

Distribution:
Innovative Logistics LLC
575 Prospect Street, Suite 301
Lakewood, NJ 08701

ISBN 978-1-927005-18-7

Printed and bound in The United States of America

<u>*Dedication*</u>

It has been an unbelievable experience working on this book and sharing my thought processes... even through this journey there have been many stumbling moments and I would revert back to what was written and say "Ki, take your own advice!" I would like to thank my publisher for encouraging me to write this book and allowing me to come into my own. They say if you are one who can count as many friends as you have fingers on your hand you are one lucky person. I am blessed to have friends who have stood by me and held my hand through some of the most difficult times I have had to go through and still stand by me. You truly know who you are... and of course my mom and children. Kaithan and Jaina, may the words I have written stay with you and guide you to continue to be successful in anything you decide to do.

-Kirin

Table of Contents

Introduction

I'm Kirin Singh and I know what you're thinking - who is this woman and why should I read her book?

Good question! And you deserve the answers. I'm a 35 year-old single mother of two and I own my own company during a time when many people are struggling to find jobs and barely surviving financially.

I'm not here to brag about that or list my accomplishments, I'm here to help. I know what it's like to be young and starting out in the world with no compass to show you the direction you should take. It's hard enough to find that first job, let alone plot a career path up the ladder to success. But you know what? It's not that it's so difficult, it's just that we tend to get steered in the wrong directions by well-meaning family, friends, and a whole system that is designed along certain lines - and those lines don't take your personal happiness and success into account.

I'm just here to share a little of my story and my philosophy, and tell you about what I know that works. Nobody can promise you a road ahead that 's perfectly straight and doesn't include any bumps along the way, but I can help you negotiate those bumps and end up ahead of the game.

My professional world is the world of real estate, so I'll be using lots of examples in that area when it comes to making specific points, but what I illustrate in the end are principles that anyone can use.

You owe it to yourself and your future to get started on the right foot. Let me help you along the way.

Chapter One

Find Who You Are - Find Your Passion

I was never one of those people who knew exactly what they wanted to be as a child. Not when it came to profession. Certainly, if you had asked me at age 10, 15, even 20 what I wanted to do "when I grow up", I would never have told you "own my own real estate company by the time I'm 35"! Yet, here I am, doing just that, happy and excited to be establishing myself in a field where I've truly found my passion.

Even so, and without a particular focus, as far back as I can remember I knew I wanted to be something. I wanted to make my mark. When I was a kid, people asked me my favourite colour, as they often do in school and so on, and other kids would say blue, pink, red - I would say orange.

People would ask me why, since it's an unusual choice, and I could never really come up with a specific reason, but now I think that it's a good way of seeing how everything has come together in my life.

Orange. It's my brand, so to speak. Orange has a warm vibrancy to it and it stands out from the crowd - it's me. It's about positive energy and constantly moving forward. I've made orange - and oranges - an integral part of my company's image, branding and message.

That's not to say that my life has been a journey of constant progress, marching steadily uphill without a misstep- far from it. I'm a hopeless romantic, and I've made more than a few stumbles in that area over the years. 'Nuff said! I've experienced many ups and downs. My life would make a great plot for a Bollywood movie. I always said I wanted to write a book; it's very cool that it's coming to fruition now, so many years later, and it's happening because I've held on to that idea no matter what else happened. As a child, I couldn't articulate what I wanted out of life, but looking back, I feel like that positive, productive orange energy is what has infused my entire professional life.

What's Your Colour?

Everyone has a colour, whether they've thought about it or not. What's yours? Your favourite colour can say a lot about your basic energy and what you bring to everything you do. Knowing what your colour - your brand - is can help you focus your efforts and find your real passion in life. Finding and developing the best of yourself and being true to that self is the real Ki to Success.

Are you a calm, healing blue? Or a fresh, creative green? I've put it in terms of colour because we all respond to it, but you can put it into any terms that you like. It's not about making a fashion statement; it's thinking about what makes you, you. What special qualities and gifts do you have to bring to the world? What qualities characterize everything that you do? Find your colour and stay true to it.

Thinking about the colour you respond to the most and your qualities as a person will also help you focus on the one big question that will make the difference between happy and unfulfilled, success and failure in your life. What do you want out of life?

MOTIVATION

What's Your Motivation?

Knowing what you want out of life means understanding your motivation. Do you want people to look up to you? Or would they smile in gratitude? What makes you happy? There's no absolute answer, right or wrong. It's about finding the right answer for you.

When you were a child, were you happiest leading the pack on a wild adventure in the woods, or were you the one making sure the smaller kids kept up at the back of the line? If you finished an assignment in school early, did you go on to do extra work, or were you happy to take the extra time to socialize with friends? It's important, because if you were the leader of the pack, you'll never be happy stuck at the lowest rung of the corporate ladder, and if you were everybody's surrogate mom, you're not likely to feel fulfilled in a high powered corporate position that doesn't involve a lot of human interaction. When you find the right fit, however, you'll no longer have a "job", you'll have a career and a passion.

I knew I wanted to "be somebody" from a very early age. I was surrounded by successful people growing up. My mother and step father were both in real estate and doing well, so I had living, breathing examples of what it meant to be "somebody" - and all the hard work that took. It was a life they introduced me to early on.

I started in real estate when I was 15. My Stepdad had been working for 25 years for one of Canada's largest home builders, and it was the first test - and my first taste - of my sales ability. At first, I would accompany him and help out on weekends as he worked at large subdivisions which were under construction. We would be in the sales office while interested potential buyers had a look at the site and the homes already built. I served as a kind of hostess once they'd decided to come in and get more information. I'd greet them with a smile and a "Here's the price list!"

One week, my stepdad couldn't make it, so I took over the whole site all on my own. Now, I obviously didn't have a real estate license at that time, so we'd called someone higher up at the building contractor's, and, not wanting to miss a full weekend of sales, she'd said, "Figure it out. Make it happen!" That was on a Thursday, and by Saturday I was on duty at the sales office.

It was a pretty easy set up. The builder had come up with a system where they had pre-packaged home options in terms of design and details and the lots were already set up. A prospective client simply had to match an available site and a home design.

I ended up selling 7 houses that weekend. What it involved at my end was filling out a sheet, taking a cheque for $1,000 as a deposit, and then putting a yellow sticker on the diagram of the site to indicate the lot was "taken". I was 17 years old and I got about $100 for every deal I signed up. I thought that was the be all and end all!

 ### *Take advantage of the opportunities*

That early "success" was what motivated me. I got a sense of satisfaction from each deal that I signed - and I still do today. It means that I've been able to help someone reach for one of their dreams at the same time as I do mine.

It kept me going, now an ever more eager helper to my stepdad on weekends. It may sound strange to say it now, but I still didn't see real estate as part of my ultimate future. To me at the time, it was a means to an end, giving me some income and work experience. But, even in what I thought of as a temporary stopover in my professional life, I made sure to make the most out of the opportunity by learning everything I could, and doing the best job that I could.

Granted, my early push to succeed and the opportunities I took up came from my immediate background - my family. It may involve a little more work on your part, but there really are opportunities all around you once you start to look.

▶ School - from clubs to volunteer work, there are lots of ways that you can get involved at school. Try different things to see what you're good at, and what makes you happiest.

8

▶ The community - an online search or just getting out into your community can also open up doors. Public institutions like libraries can offer volunteer opportunities or links to other organizations. Are you creative? Arts organizations are always looking for a helping hand. Passionate about the environment? There are organizations looking for people like you.

▶ Get paid! - getting a job can do much more than put some money in your pocket. When you're young and inexperienced, the choice of jobs on offer may not nticing. Your dream position probably doesn't involve flipping burgers or picking up litter at the park, but think of it this way: every job can teach you something, whether it involves social or practical skills, or finding out about how businesses run. Learn what you can.

It's never too soon to start thinking about your direction

Boyfriends and partying may seem like much more fun than thinking about your future, especially when it seems like you have so much time. But planning ahead doesn't mean you have to give up your whole social life and all your other interests. Quite the contrary.

If you take the time to find out about your interests and what you're good at, and find your motivation, it will be how you'll want to spend your time. That's the real magic of finding your direction in life - it's like settling into your natural groove.

Don't let it be about fear, and don't think of it as something hanging over your head - a mysterious "future" you somehow have to sort out right now or else. It's about making positive steps in finding your place in the world. But how do you go about doing that? And how do you start from scratch? Here are some ideas:

▶ ***What are you good at?***
Everyone is good at something! If you haven't found your unique skill or talent yet, then explore until you do. That could mean signing up for dance class or volunteering at the hospital. What are/were your best subjects in school? Once you find your special gift, it may or may not seem to immediately lead to any kind of practical use. If you're a talented musician, the possibilities are obvious, but if you're great at telling jokes, then what? A career in stand -up comedy certainly isn't for everyone. That's where some creative thinking kicks in. If you're good at telling jokes, then you're good at telling stories and

communicating. You like to stand out in the crowd by entertaining others, and you know how to get their attention with words. Those skills can translate into a multitude of career pursuits and possibilities.

▶ *What do you want to be good at?*

You don't have to settle for what you know right here and now. Take a trip down the lane of possibility and see what you find. What dreams do you have, what do you fantasize about doing? If you're drawn to a particular field or activity, it's probably with good reason, and that reason might just be a latent talent waiting to be discovered. Don't hesitate to follow your fantasies when they lead you down a path of learning and growth. Even if you don't find exactly what you're looking for, you're sure to benefit from the experience.

▶ *What excites you?*

Your own feelings - good or bad - will be a good indicator of where your talents and passions lie. Do you get angry when you hear about cruelty to animals or damage to the environment? Strong feelings are a plus and a necessity if you want to educate people about issues, help raise funds, or help to organize events for a non-profit group, for example.

▶ ***Start with what - and who - you know***

In sales, your trainers will tell you to begin by approaching people you know. It only makes sense. You already have a rapport via your existing relationship, and presumably there are levels of trust and an established mode of communication. You'll find it easier to talk to them, and to approach them. The same logic can work in reverse, when you're looking for ideas. If you're stuck on figuring out what to look into or how to find a vocation , talent or interest, start by looking at your circle of family and friends. What special skills do they have? What jobs do they do? Is it something that seems of interest? Then ask - and listen. At the very worst, you'll learn something. At best, it might fire up your own interest and maybe even get you a potential mentor who can help show you the ropes.

Once I'd finished high school, my family urged me to get my real estate license. My mother, brother and step father were already working in the field. It wasn't my first choice, or what I thought of as my "dream career", but I was making money and was bitten by the bug of early success. I was already studying Early Childhood Education with dreams of opening daycare centres, but if I wanted to open my own daycare centre (or centres) then I would need money to get started, that was a certainty. I'll freely admit that my background also influenced me here; I grew up in a fairly affluent household, and I'd gotten used to having my own money from working for years at that point. So at the time, real estate seemed an ideal means to an end, and I ended up putting my daycare dreams on hold. I decided to go ahead and study real estate and write the exam at the same time. Let's just say I was not an overnight sensation! I failed the Phase One exam the first time I wrote it, and my parents made it clear that they were less than thrilled.

It taught me something. Because I saw the real estate exam as a sideline that I was doing under pressure from my family, I hadn't really put my mind to it. I'd put in what I thought of as an adequate effort, and left it at that. But the results didn't thrill me either. So, I went back into it, this time determined to do a good job, and I did - I passed and got my license.

Persistence Pays Off

There is always a way from A to B. If you want something, there is always a way to get it - but, the road may not be straight and it may not come easy all the time. I'd done pretty well in the real estate world already by the time I was done high school, but as I found out, it didn't mean that the exam was a push over.

Early failures are a blessing and an advantage, and here's why:

- They force you to regroup, re-evaluate and come at the task again.

- They teach you how to be diligent and work at something until it's accomplished.

- They can point out skills or knowledge that you lack.

All in all, they point you in the direction of the solution, whether that involves putting in more hours or effort, more practise, education or research. Think of it not as a failure but as a correction to your path, one that offers a solution you can then implement. Being able to stick to a path or plan until you get results will be a key element to your future successes, and you'll come to expect that the road will always have its ups, downs and nasty potholes to navigate. Taking each "failure" as a way of fine tuning your course turns them into stepping stones along your path to success.

Discipline - It's not sexy, but it's for real

I felt a sense of accomplishment when I got my license, even though everyone I knew was in University doing their thing. I'd gone straight to the Ontario Real Estate Association...but I was now a Real Estate agent. It was kind of cool. That sense of accomplishment went beyond whether or not my heart was really in real estate. It was a sense of having completed something, and having accomplished something by the sheer dint of hard work. I'd put in the hours studying, and it paid off. I was learning that discipline can be rewarding.

It sounds like something your parents - or grandparents! - go on about, those good old fashioned values. But let's forget about the rest of the world and think about you. Think of discipline as your friend. It's what will get you through a tough workload and smooth over difficult situations. It will be a mainstay of your professional career, when people are depending on you to deliver goods or services at a specific quality and/or level. It will get you through ups and downs in your life and your work. I can tell you from experience that having a disciplined approach to a career can even help you through difficult and dark moments in your personal life. It's an essential life skill.

Enthusiasm is the key

Where do you come up with the strength to be so disciplined? Some people, it's true, are simply more stoic by nature, and will find persevering comes naturally - but we're not talking about having the discipline to put up with a dreary existence or conditions that are less that satisfying on a permanent basis. We're talking about having the discipline to see your dreams through to completion. There's a big difference.

Discipline works for you when it leads you in a positive direction, and here's where it loops back to the beginning: your motivation. When you find what motivates you, what really lights your fire and enthusiasm, then the discipline part will come easy. When you work at what you love, it's not like work at all. Every day begins with enthusiasm for what you're doing and where you're going, and the bumps along the way may slow you down a little, but they all turn out fine in the end because you never lose sight of what is driving you.

Finding your passion is essential because success is a lot of work! You'll need something to keep you going, and passion and the motivation it inspires are what will do the trick.

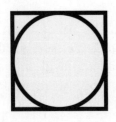

What's Your Natural Fit?

I am definitely a schmoozer! I love people, and that's what I love about what I do. People get turned off of the idea of getting into a sales position because they only associate it with that "hard sales" cliché. You know, the obnoxious car salesman who won't take no for an answer, and pushes you into buying something that you don't want, don't need and/or can't afford.

But that's not what I discovered at all. Sales is about communication, about establishing a rapport with your prospective client and then finding out how you can fulfill their needs and situation. I'm a natural communicator and I simply began by talking, by telling stories and learning how to really listen to what others have to say too. Everything else - including getting the prospective client to sign on the dotted line and become a client for real - came from that.

I love the idea of helping people reach their goals, and educating them on matters about which, sadly, so many people in our society are completely ignorant. Sales, and as it turns out, real estate sales, is a natural fit for me, something I would never have predicted. I just went with the opportunity and made the most of it, and in the process I found something I'm good at.

You'll know when you find your own "natural fit". It'll be something that speaks to your personality and makes you feel good about yourself. You'll feel like you're doing just what you're supposed to be doing. It will involve your passion, so that the work itself will motivate you to keep going. You'll feel a great level of enthusiasm about your job.

Maybe you do like the party lifestyle - maybe that really does seem like your passion in life. Think about what exactly draws you to it. Is it the socializing, the schmoozing, keeping up with your friends and making new ones? Is it the fun of getting dressed up in a chic cocktail dress and glitzy jewellery? Or do you have fun planning your own parties and events, getting all the right elements and people together and then watching a great night unfold? All of those individual interests can point the way to a passion and lead to many career possibilities. There are many positions in the fields of public relations, media and broadcasting where going to parties is part of the job!

Getting there won't be about partying, though, and that's where you have to be able to use your head. If that's what makes you happy and feel fulfilled in life, then pursue it and put in the work that it takes to get to that position. That's where the perseverance and discipline come in. You have to be able to put in the work today that will get you where you want to go tomorrow, and there's no substitute for putting in the hours. The pay off, though, will be more than worth your investment. Trust me on that!

Turn Negatives Into Positives

− vs +

My mother and father split up when I was about six years old. It was a very acrimonious divorce and a torturous experience for me as a kid. There was a prolonged period of a lot of strife - lots of calls to the police, fighting and other disruptions. My father withdrew from the situation in the end, and I was largely raised by my Step Father. My brother was older and branched more on his own, leaving me to deal with our home life more or less by myself. I responded like many children do, by acting out. I had some issues in childhood; I was a compulsive liar and attention seeker.

Those aren't qualities I'd be proud of today, but I can also say that those impulses are still part of my "orange" personality. The compulsive lying didn't come from a desire to hide the truth, but to embellish it. Channelled in a positive direction, towards truth instead of falsehood, that impulse became my gift for the gab, a way of telling stories and engaging my clients. Instead of getting attention by acting out, I've learned to get it by offering something of value, the message about financial smarts that I've begun to share with the rest of the world. I've taken that message to the public by doing radio and media interviews, educational programs and, in fact, by writing this book.

The point is, you should work with everything available to you - including your own faults. Faults in character come from impulses, those very same motivations that we've been talking about. If you can figure out the motivation behind negative behaviour, then you can turn it into something positive and productive.

Don't Settle Too Soon

Follow your passion once you find it, but at the same time, don't be so tightly focused that you don't give yourself time to expand, grow and learn. Keep an open mind. After I got my license in April of 1998, I opened my very first site, working for the same builder my Stepdad had worked with for so long. It was a brand new subdivision, and I sold 24 townhouses that very first day I was open for business - what felt like my business, even though technically, I was still working for someone else.

When you get a taste of money and you're 19, 20 years old, it's pretty cool, that's for sure. I had my own place, my own car, and a professional life that was on the way up. That was more than enough motivation for me to start out with. I worked for the same company for six years, signing deal after deal under pretty much the same circumstances.

My mother is a brilliant business woman and worked in real estate herself. She became my most important mentor during that period. Apart from the art of making sales for the company, she showed me how to find my way around the world of real estate and make money on my own. I started buying and then flipping properties at a profit, becoming adept at finding the bargains, those "gems in the rough" that could be fixed up and sold quickly.

Everything was going great, except... I was living on my own, in my own condo, and then going to work in a model home every day, again completely on my own. As a natural schmoozer and people person, too much solitary living and working was making me chafe at the bit. I ended up getting bored, and losing some of the spark I'd had in the beginning.

So I decided to make a change. I quit my job with the builder and decided to go backpacking in Europe for three months - something wild and unstructured, and not like anything I'd done before. And I loved it!

Challenge Yourself

After doing so much talking about finding your one passion and honing in on it, here comes the caveat: if you don't broaden your horizons and keep growing as a person, there are strengths, interests and passions you may just miss out on. You might feel, as I did starting out, that you've found your true calling and you want to get started on your career path right away - but how do you know about what you haven't tried yet?

Travel is an incredible experience no matter what age you are, but when you're young and just starting out in life, it can take on particular significance. It enlarges your world, and lets you see how other people live and work. It gives you a broader perspective. I was traveling and learning about history at the same time, surrounded by the incredible architecture and culture of Europe.

Perhaps most importantly, it brings out your self-reliance. You have to make sure you're at the train station or airport on time, and figure out how to find your way in a strange city when you don't speak the language. You have to sort out getting food in your stomach and a roof over your head on the fly. I would encourage anyone to travel when they're young, and I know a trip is something I'll give to my own children when they're ready. It's an experience that strengthens your backbone. These are all qualities you need in business, or any field that requires a self-starting approach.

 ### *Education Beyond School*

Travel is a great example of the kind of experience that educates you in ways that schooling and formal education can't. Just when you thought all that "learning" was over, you realize it's a lifelong deal! Whether you

22

choose to physically leave town or not, be sure to explore your world as far as you can. Try new things and meet new people - you never know what you might find, or find out.

There are many things, including essential life skills, that you'll never learn about in the classroom. You might be apprehensive about the unknown, or maybe those first few pay checks feel so good that you just want to settle in, afraid to jeopardize what you see as a good thing by taking a chance. That's a natural way to feel. We all want security, and will most often take the choice that seems to offer the most of it.

But, you'll be selling yourself short, and losing out on potential opportunities, if you don't continue to learn and grow. Your motivation and direction in life will go from positive progress to empty stagnation. You don't have to settle! It's possible to have it all - success and happiness, or more importantly, the happiness that comes from a career you love, which is the ultimate success.

Finances and learning how to handle them are a vital part of being able to function as an adult in our world, yet it's one of those things we all have to learn on our own. They should be teaching financial responsibility in high school, but we're left to navigate those often confusing waters entirely without guidance from the school system. It's no wonder that so many people today are drowning in debt and living from pay check to pay check - no one has taught them how to build their finances. Growing up in such a business savvy family, it seemed completely crazy to me, and it still does.

Setting Myself Apart From the Rest

As a child, I wanted to stand out from the crowd, and as an adult, in the field that I thought of as a convenient sideline, I found a way that I could. Once I realized how little the general public knew about the true value of real estate and building lasting wealth, it ignited a passion I never knew I had for teaching, for spreading the word.

Now, there are many other real estate professionals and entire companies, in fact, who offer educational seminars and other learning opportunities. I looked into some of the leading providers of real estate education in my area, and found that, in one case, a company's own research showed that 80% of the people who took their seminars walked away without buying a thing. They saw it as "research" - but in reality they still don't know where to start.

The way I figured out how to be different was to offer not only the theory, but a practical application of it. I begin all my sales presentations by making the same kinds of points that all the educational seminars make to establish the value and pure common sense of investing in real estate. But then I add one crucial step: I'll say, "Okay, now that we've talked about the theory, I have a few properties for you to look at." I give them concrete advice about the kinds of properties they should be considering and the price range that will be comfortable for them to maintain. I'll tell them what areas they should consider buying in, and why.

I never wanted to "educate" just for the sake of airing out a theory. I wanted it to have real and practical applications, and make a real difference to the clients I serve. I make sure that the process not only makes sense, it becomes doable. Once they've been shown how "doable" it is, they buy. It really is as simple as that.

My entire business is word of mouth. That's probably the hugest compliment you can give anyone, and I know it's because of the passion and commitment I bring to the table. I believe 100% in what I'm doing and what I'm selling my clients, and look forward to each day at work. I still get a charge out of signing each deal, and I've found a creative and productive use of my natural gifts.

To review, these are the themes that we've talked about so far, and that I'll enlarge on throughout this book:

- Find your passion.

- Stick with it.

- Learn to work at it.

- Keep growing at the same time, learning as much as you can.

- Find a way to make your own mark by taking advantage of the opportunities you find.

Life can be a rewarding journey, or just making time. Just remember - you alone hold the keys to your success.

Chapter Two

Starting Out

$\mathcal{S}$tarting out on my own as a professional woman was a very exciting time for me. I felt charged up and ready to make a name for myself. When I came back from Europe after my eye-opening trip, it was a really proud year. I turned 25 in November, and I had always said I wanted to own my own detached home by that age. I moved into my own place on November 1st and my birthday was the 22nd - I turned 25, and I felt like I was on the way up, independent, and taking on the world on my own terms. There's nothing like that first time you look around and realize everything you see is yours from the carpets to the dishes and that cool bedspread that matches the blue of your bedroom walls. It all belongs to you and you got it by working hard.

I knew back then that I wanted to "be something" but I didn't know what exactly that would be. My mother was already a successful real estate agent, working under the umbrella of a large multi-national real estate company. Since I already had experience in the field, I decided to go back to it. I went to work as an independent sales professional out of the same office as my Mom.

Many people work with family in one way or another; it can go incredibly well, or it can be excruciating. My mother had gotten to the level of success that she had by being a perfectionist. She expected a lot of herself, and set herself elevated goals that she'd work hard to reach. She could be just as hard of others, and she was really, really hard on me -which she should have been. I know she didn't want me to become one of those privileged children whose parents worked hard only to raise children who didn't understand the value of it because they'd had everything handed to them on a proverbial silver platter. She knew the joy of earning rewards for her efforts - both tangible and intangible - and she wanted to pass that down to me. Still working within the same company, I ended up dealing directly with one of their top agents in the province, and he became a huge mentor to me. Even though I'd already been working in the field, I realized that I still had a lot to learn not only about the real estate business specifically, but about business dealings in the professional world in general. Moreover, it was the kind of knowledge I couldn't get from books or by going back to school.

Mentors and Role Models

Some businesses and trades have a formal mentoring system, but most often, it'll be up to you to find a mentor or role model to follow. Why is it important? As my own example and experience illustrates, there are many aspects of working life and your chosen profession that you simply can't anticipate or prepare for by reading up the latest literature or by getting an A in class. In my business, real estate, a huge factor that essentially determines your entire success or failure in the field will be your sales ability, closely linked to your ability to communicate and connect with people - i.e. your future sales prospects. You can take a hundred courses in real estate and they won't prepare you for the real life situations you'll encounter when you're sitting face to face with another human being who may (or may not!) want to buy what you have to sell.

Those are often called "soft skills" or people skills. They're hard to evaluate, because everyone has their own unique style and way of approaching them. They'd be hard to mark, in other words - success is the only proof of what works. From my boss and my mother's example, I was working on and refining my way of communicating with clients, how to present myself and my whole sales presentation.

Find a Mentor

Even without a formal mentoring system, you can get the same experience by finding someone you can look up to professionally. That may mean someone who works at the same place you do, or if not then someone who works in the same field. Approach them and ask if they'd mind mentoring you, and perhaps if time is a consideration, if they'd simply be available occasionally for professional advice.

▶ Find someone who is where you'd like to be in ten years or more.

▶ Think not only of whether they're successful, but how? - i.e. are they known for being ethical and fair in their dealings - or for cutting corners and fly by night deals? Do other people regard them the way you'd like to be regarded?

▶ If there's no one suitable or available at work, then look for other places you can find people in your profession - maybe professional associations or organizations, universities or colleges with programs in your field. Face to face meetings are wonderful, but you can also have a very effective professional mentoring relationship with someone online or on the phone.

Once you've got a good role model and someone who's willing to show you the ropes, don't be afraid to make good use of the opportunity. Older professionals are most often very willing and may even feel honoured to pass along the benefit of their years of experience and expertise. I can tell you myself that passing along knowledge you've acquired "the hard way" is hugely rewarding and can bring a lot of satisfaction. It takes what you've learned from hard work and adds a new dimension - you're giving back.

When you're the one starting out, the first step is to recognize how much you don't know, as funny as that may sound. Never assume that you already know how it's done.

▶ Ask lots of questions - the only mistake is to not ask when you should.

▶ It's not just about the ins and outs of work, but about professional life in general. How do they approach it? What makes them different than the others, what sets them apart in terms of behaviour or approach?

I promise you'll learn loads of things that will help you navigate your way through the workplace. The thing is, knowing your job is one thing. Knowing your way around the office (or factory, or school, or wherever you find yourself) is quite another. High tech internet based companies, for example, often have a very casual corporate culture, where jeans and t-shirts are the norm, there's a Foosball table in the staff room and everyone checks Twitter constantly from their company issued smart phone. On the other hand, you may find yourself in an insurance company with a strict dress code and separate washrooms for management and regular staff. It's not just a matter of showing up in Brooks Brothers while everyone else is in yoga pants and jeans, or a matter of fitting in for the sake of fitting in. It's about recognizing what the company's image and message is all about, and then finding your way and your place in it.

I learned some essential lessons from my first mentors, ones that have stayed with me and informed my entire professional life. I learned what success is really about and what having ambition really means. There are about a zillion teenage girls who want to be a "star" and a pop singing idol along the lines of Lady Gaga or Katy Perry, and it's not even about how many actually make it to the top - how many even get started along the way? You can want and desire success in any field you enter, but to achieve it, you really have to put yourself on the line and make a whole effort. That's what ambition is all about. You put yourself out there every chance and in every way you can and reach for that prize. You have to go after it wholeheartedly.

While I was working with my new mentor, my mother left the company and set up a firm of her own with my brother. Eventually, I too left the company and went to work with my mother and my brother -my older brother who was already that much farther along in the field. Now... if I'd found working in the same office as my mother a taxing experience, then imagine what it was like to work with two members of my success-driven family, and as the youngest and most inexperienced family member at that. It's tough enough to start out at the bottom of the totem pole without the upper rungs of it made up of people who know you inside out, including all your faults!

Getting Along At Work

A challenge is always an opportunity, though, and I can say this for sure: the experience of working with my family taught me a great deal about how to get along with others in a working environment. I have to admit that a lot of what follows came from learning it the hard way, but passing along the well-earned knowledge is part of what makes that worthwhile.

Whether or not you work with family, it's most likely that you'll be working with others in some capacity or perhaps even in a work group. Even if you work on your own or only deal with others via the internet or other arm's length medium, at some point, you'll have to deal with people and it may not always work out the way you'd like to. You may find yourself at odds with someone else's work style or pace, or their way of communicating, for example. Being able to get along with others in a professional context is an essential skill.

▶ **Keep personal and business matters separate** - I know it can be hard, but if you go out to lunch with a girlfriend from work and she offends you with an off colour or insulting remark, you can't let it affect you later in the day when you're both at a project meeting. Likewise, I had to remember that even if my Mom critiqued my sales presentation in what I felt was an overly harsh manner, I still had to show up on Sunday for brunch.

- **Make it about the work and focus on the job at hand, not the person** - If you keep your eye on the ball, so to speak, and frame everything around work during work hours, then you'll find it easier to keep the two relationships distinct. That's good advice that really applies to a wide range of working environments and situations. You may be negotiating a good lease rate on an office space and find yourself with a personal dislike of the agent you have to deal with, one of those situations where the other person just rubs you the wrong way. Do you let it affect your lease negotiations? Of course not! You can have a good rant over the agent's rude behaviour or overwhelming cologne with your girlfriends after work; for the moment, focus only on the figures and the facts of the lease.

- **A special note for internet communications** - Take the time to make sure that your words also focus on the work and avoid personal references - they can be so easily taken the wrong way. Make your language neutral, i.e. avoid emotion-laden words and phrasings, and express your thoughts in factual rather than opinionated terms. Try to be as clear as you can at all times, and don't forget that a little politeness and consideration can go a long way towards maintaining good will.

Keep it on an objective level - That's your overall goal. It can be very hard to take your personal feelings out of your business dealings, but the closer you can get to objectivity, the better off you'll be in many ways. It will obviously allow you to be more efficient at work, but it will also save your sanity by preserving a separate space for your personal life and feelings.

Fix the issues and follow the right channels as necessary - When it comes to workplace conflicts, focus on fixing the issues in question and offer logical solutions. Even if the other person is behaving like a completely unreasonable egotist, approaching it in a professional manner and following the appropriate channels will leave them with no argument against you or what you're proposing - and your superiors will notice that too. Keeping your cool will de-escalate personal conflicts.

Leave your ego out of it - This is a really important

lesson, but one some people never learn! Life - and work - aren't about winning every little skirmish that fate tosses your way. It's about keeping your eye on the ball and going for a win in the long run. That becomes so much easier if you can leave your ego out of the equation. That means you won't sweat it if your co-worker's design is the one your boss decides to go with, despite the fact that it doesn't incorporate all the elements she asked for and yours does... Instead, you'll focus on doing the best job you can in the role you're assigned and then working towards the next opportunity to shine. Believe me if I tell you you're doing yourself a favour and saving yourself a lot of aggravation if you can follow this rule.

Take time outside work - When working with family or friends, focus on the task at hand during the work hours, but be sure to make time for that out of work relationship too. A lot of what I've said here has focused on how to get along at work and depersonalizing your interactions with others, but if you have a relationship outside of work hours, then you have to put the time and effort into that too. Whether you do something special or just hang out at home in front of the TV, make every minute count in a way that is decidedly not "work related".

Keep learning - it's not enough to coast

So, you've got yourself started in a career and you've even got a mentor who's helping you along with the finer points of the game. A few years have gone by, so now you can sit back and take it easy, or at least easier, right? You're firmly on the way up…

In reality, the farther you go along the road to professional success, the more you understand that there's always something to learn, and that even what you learn needs to be updated and upgraded. The thing is, the more you know about your field, the more opportunities will open up to you, and the better you'll be able to find your ideal role within it.

In my case, I got started in real estate because it was easy for me - my family was already well established in that world. It wasn't only encouraged, you could say I was pretty much pushed into it, although sticking with it and making it a real career was, in the end, my own choice. Things started out well, but even beyond the practical lessons I was getting via mentors and what I encountered at work on a regular basis, I wanted to go on to learn everything I could.

Set Yourself Apart

In real estate, among other things, they teach you about the ins and outs of different types of construction and building systems and the marketplace, including the effects of location, location, location on price. For me, though, it went beyond that, and I wanted to look at the role real estate plays in our lives in various ways. Tying all of those threads together, I began to realize how important it was to both creating and solidifying wealth. I learned about the real value of real estate - well beyond basic ideas about buying low and selling high, making profits and making a deal that look good on a balance sheet.

I saw that society is made up of rich and of poor, and the only real difference between the two groups is the way they handle their funds. I saw that virtually any solvent middle class person can invest in real estate, as the rich and upper classes in former eras have been doing for as long as there has been western society. It has real and enduring value and it never fails to bring returns over the long haul. When you use it in a smart and deliberate way, it can help to finance itself as it grows in value. When I came to realize that anyone could do it, I felt passionate about teaching other people about it, and it became the way I distinguished myself from anyone else in my field. That kind of educational approach is the cornerstone of my business and business practices.

It was learning more about my field that ignited my true passion and interest in it.

Explore the Possibilities

I was learning and growing and doing my best at real estate, but still... I had those dreams about opening up daycare centres. Since I was still young and didn't want to turn my back on my "first love" just yet, in 2004, I decided to leave the world of real estate -knowing I could always come back to it - and explore the world of early childhood education.

I left real estate entirely and worked as a Kindergarten teacher for a whole year, following that dream as I kept my real estate licence. But even on the surface, I wasn't like the other teachers; I drove a Lexus to work and had my own house. The parents of my young students would chat, and after finding out my background, they'd ask me, "Why are you teaching children??"

Still, I adored it. I love children and I always have. I was also getting married at the time and thinking about having my own children, so it was great preparation for that experience. Even though I didn't stay in that field and decided to go back to real estate, it was a time I enjoyed and remember fondly.

- ▶ Leave no stone unturned - even if you're set on one way, make time to explore other paths while you're young. If you feel like you're heart's really in it, then go for it - or you'll always wonder what it was like.

- ▶ There may very well be more than one "good fit" for you in terms of career or field. Growing up is about finding a path by working towards something that's realistic as well as fulfilling, and that may involve checking out more than one type of position.

- ▶ Is money important to you? There's no shame in it! You can't make it your number one priority because all alone, it won't make you happy, but if a certain kind of lifestyle is important to you, then you'll never feel fulfilled in a job that doesn't offer the opportunity to make more than a basic living.

- ▶ Is advancement important? Then you have to have a position that can lead to more or you'll be easily bored and feel stifled before too long.

- ▶ There may be more than one single possibility. Don't become obsessed with one job or single position -

there may be many more ways than one to get what you want, and your key to finding that out is to keep exploring and learning as you go along.

You'll find out what really matters to you

After a year, I realized that, while I loved working with kids, I'd gotten used to a certain income and a lifestyle that I would not be able to sustain as a Kindergarten teacher or involved in the Early Childhood Education field as a teacher.

It was an important lesson - discovering the difference between my dream and the reality. Some positions just don't offer the kind of financial opportunities that others do routinely. That's reality. When you're trying to decide what field and what role within it will appeal to you and ignite your own passion there are a number of factors that can come into play.

▶ **Security vs versatility in terms of a career** - Many people get talked into a basic 9 to 5 lifestyle because of the security of a regular pay check along with benefits like dental and prescription coverage, but over time they find themselves bored and unfulfilled, and work becomes a chore. You can't succeed by default. If you're not into it, it will only ever be "just a job" and it won't lead to the kind of life you want. There are plenty of people who make a good living without all those guarantees - an even better than good living, but you need to be able to deal with ups and downs, and be a self-starter. There is always a trade-off, in other words, and you have to decide which way is for you.

- **Lead, follow or on your own?** - You need to find a good fit for your role. If you're a leader, then you'll want opportunities for advancement and management positions. If you'd rather be a supportive player, that's a crucial role too, but you'll want to find one that fits your talents. How would your gifts and skills be best put to good use? If you're best working as the lone wolf, then maybe a consulting or contractual role is the way for you.

- **Work environment** - Do you love the familiarity of your own cubicle or office with plants and photographs of your favourite people or pets? Do you like the water cooler chats and knowing your work mates day in and day out? Or do you get off on meeting new people every day and finding your way in different work places and situations? It's important!

Work is how you'll spend the majority of your time and the way it takes place will make the difference between long term contentment and fulfillment and simmering frustration.

Your individual choices on all these matters will depend on your personality, and that's where the experimentation comes into it. Take the time and opportunity to find out about yourself by acting on your ideas and dreams. You can't know what makes you happy until you've tried various things.

Learning to deal with life's ups and downs

I mentioned meeting my husband and getting engaged during the time I spent as a Kindergarten teacher. By the time I went back to real estate, major events in my personal life were coming thick and fast. I got married and my son was born in the same year, just after I left teaching. My daughter was born two years later. Then a year after that, tragedy struck my life when my Stepdad passed away.

When he passed away, my soul kind of opened up. Everything came into perspective and I was forced to re-evaluate everything. Was I really happy? Did I feel fulfilled with my life as it was? What was really important to me?

I was forced to realize that while my husband was a great guy and a great father, he just wasn't that great for me. We didn't get along on a day to day basis, and the foundations of the relationship were coming apart at the seams. He did not come from the same culture as I did. With my more traditional East Indian background, we had to fight to be together - one of the reasons that made it so hard to admit that the end of the relationship had come. We'd gone through so much, it was hard to hear "I told you so!" And so the situation had lingered longer than it should have.

I tried everything to work it out, but somehow, my Stepfather's illness and passing away and the profound effect that had on me gave me the strength to see the truth. It just wasn't working. On top of that, I knew that if I wanted to achieve what I wanted to in the world of real estate and do it "my way", I would have to leave the family business and strike out on my own. Within months of his funeral, I'd left both my husband and my job with my mother and brother.

I was starting over from scratch, and it didn't come easy. There were a lot of hard feelings on both sides, and the inevitable disruption to not only my life, but my children's lives too. It was a very difficult time for all of us, but I learned a lot about surviving the roller coaster of life.

You Can't Avoid It

Difficult times come to everyone's life; I'm certainly not unique in that regard. How you handle those ups and downs is what will make the difference.

- During times of change and uncertainty at home, remember that your job and career can be your best friend - the one solid thing in your life when your personal life and/or relationships go south.

- Keep your chin up and keep up appearances in terms of looking good and looking after yourself. As funny as it may sound, keeping up appearances will help you keep it together for real. Act like everything's okay, and it will begin to feel okay too.

- Again it's about keeping work and personal life separate to some degree. As hard as it may seem, you can't let last night's fight with your boyfriend or even a big break up in a serious relationship get you off your rhythm in every other aspect of your life. Use the opportunity to focus on what is working out rather than what is not, on the rewarding relationships rather than the failing one.

- Give yourself time - just get through one day at a time and let the future happen along the way. Once you've got some time and perspective, you'll see that your feelings have cooled and your attitudes have changed.

- Stick to the basics - taking care of yourself by eating right and getting enough sleep is more important to maintaining your mood and overall productivity than you think.

- Give yourself a treat - something that's good for you, and something you can afford. Maybe a new hairstyle or a visit to the spa with give you a bit of a lift and help you get through a rough patch.

There's no special formula for getting over rough times in your life, and they may change your ideas and values, as they did mine. You can use them, as I did, to re-evaluate your direction in life and work and make the changes you need to, and in that sense you'll turn a negative into a positive force in your life. In the end, my Stepfather's death was so pivotal it led me to realign my priorities and step out in a new direction all together. It was scary - but also exhilarating.

Hopefully it doesn't take a tragic event to get you to make that kind of evaluation. It's an entirely natural process.

What it means is, you're never "done" - you don't ever reach a point where everything is perfect and just stays that way all the time. Every so often in life, you have to re-evaluate your direction and ask yourself: are you happy? Are you fulfilled? Are you doing what you should be doing in life? As painful as it may be sometimes, if you're not, you have to make changes and move on.

Life isn't about finding one ideal path and walking in a straight line forever. You have to be prepared to roll with the punches and keep going even when the going gets tough.

Once I decided to open up my own real estate company and be my own boss, I let my ambitions soar. My goal is to be the biggest real estate brokerage - worldwide! When I am, I'll give back and build schools and daycare centres - that's still my passion too.

I've mentioned that I had a feeling from a young age that I wanted to "be somebody". I'd learned about myself along the way. I knew that I liked to be able to make as much money as my work afforded me rather than be what it felt like to me as "stuck" on a fixed salary. I wanted the freedom to make as much as I could - but I also wanted to help people, to educate them, and yes, to work with children at some point too. So what do I want? I want it all!

I think I have two sides to my personality. I'm the success oriented sales person and I'm also a great communicator who loves to reach out to people, to help and to educate. I've managed to incorporate both of those sides in my ambitions, and leave some room in the future to add working with or for children in some capacity.

That's the way you'll find a "good fit" for you. Sometimes, depending on the circumstances, it may involve working at one thing and having another passion that you'll develop on the side, like me. Maybe you'll take art lessons and show your paintings in gallery shows on the side while you work at a bank. You might volunteer with a children's charity or belong to a music group. The balance of work and life is really the balance of life itself - if you're realistic and work at all of it, you really can have it all.

Become who you want to be - successful!

From the time I first opened the doors of my own office, my work ethic developed around how I want and need to approach it. I always have music on, because it energizes me. I stand strong, and always try to stand tall in my posture. When I slump, I feel different. I feel less capable, not as strong and confident. When I stand tall, I feel like I'm going to win - and I do.

I always wear business clothes, even if I'm spending the day on my own filling out paperwork or doing research. I'm trying to project that I'm serious about what I do, no matter what. The fact is that people judge people by what they see, and in business situations, you often don't have the time or opportunity to get a deeper understanding.

Having said that, from a business point of view, no matter what the situation, it's a good idea to try to look deeper than that first impression in your potential customers. At one time, I was going to buy a car and I had my eyes on a luxury model. I was bringing $30,000 in cash but I didn't take any time over my appearance and showed up to the showroom in t-shirt and jeans. Well, let's just say that the salesman's reception was less than friendly; in fact, he treated me like dirt, completely judging me by my bargain basement look on that day. I was heartbroken and upset, and was complaining about it to a cousin over the phone. He suggested a different car dealership and I took my cash there and sure enough, they were great with me and made the sale. The next day, I drove back to the luxury car dealership to show him how he'd lost the sale!

The moral of the story is, look the part so you make the right impression in other people's eyes, but at the same time, you need to be smart enough to know yourself that looks aren't everything. Sometimes, a less than glamorous or stylish look is exactly what you want. I bought a computer from a well-known dealership and manufacturer, and while I was shopping in the branded store, I was impressed by the fact that all their sales personnel had a very "average" look. No one was particularly well dressed, and no one could pass for a runway model. However, that strategy suited the purposes of the manufacturer very well. That was their pitch, their appeal - we're just like you, the customer. If we can be experts and use this computer, then you can too.

Along with projecting my own professional image and that of my new company, I was hiring other people for the first time. I had to think about how I'd approach that, and I knew that I had to insist that anyone I worked with had to believe in the same philosophy about real estate and its value. They had to, if they were to fulfill the role that I had conceived. First off the bat is that my business focuses on investment properties, so I stipulate that any agent who works for me has to buy investment properties themselves. They can't sell it if they don't know it and believe it themselves, that's just the way I think.

Those first few years were tough, eventful -and exciting. I'd been through a lot but learned so much.

Chapter Three

Growing Up

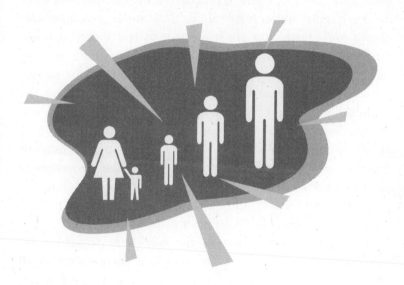

*W*hat is our purpose in life? Do you believe in destiny?
Do we create our own destiny? Do we have any control?

I ask myself that all the time.

Never mind the big questions - more often I'm thinking can
I not just get through one year without the bullshit? I've
gone through my share of upheaval and it felt terrible at the
time, but one thing I've learned as I've gone along is this:
everyone deals with ups and downs. Nobody's life is perfect.
Still, I know from experience that it can be especially hard

to look around during those moments when you think life isn't going so great and see people around you who seem to have it all under control. Real estate is a competitive world and those who are successful in it are conspicuous; in fact, I've worked with some of the best of them, the top salespeople in the area. I was always surrounded by people who inspired me to do well by example. They gave me something to shoot for, but it meant that sometimes I was all too aware of how far I had to go!

The "success" I'm talking about can be in any field or however you define it, from getting your first gallery show as a painter to making your first multi-million dollar sale in real estate. It certainly doesn't have to involve money, but in our world, that's always a primary concern.

When you're starting out in the world in particular, it's easy to look around you and feel like there's some kind of gap or even a wall between where you are and where you want to be; a wall between you and the mysterious world inhabited by successful people. Sometimes you feel like you can try and try over and over as many times and as hard as you like, but you'll never be able to figure out how to scale that wall.

You look at people who are successful and you think, are they just lucky? Were they born under the right stars so that everything came easily to them?

Maybe it's just me.

Of course it's not "just you"

It may seem tempting at times to think that way. There's just something about me that won't let me be as successful as those people around me. It even becomes a kind of excuse for not trying, and accepting a much lesser role in life than you are capable of. Don't listen to that "inner voice" and let yourself give in to fear. Fear will make you shy away from the very challenges that will bring your best rewards.

I think you need to take on life as an adventure, and to keep your perspective fresh, it's good to ask yourself those big questions from time to time. As you get older and progress through the various stages of your life your answers may change and develop over time, and you'll begin to realize that you have an incredible amount of control over one particular aspect - in fact, in this area you're in charge 100%. That aspect is you.

Success may seem very far away at the moment. You may even feel like there are forces - family pressures, business constraints, a lack of education or qualifications - very real forces that are holding you back and standing in your way. But people don't become successful because everything was made easy for them by some lucky chance or because they were born into situations that put every circumstance into just the right place. They become successful because they worked at it and didn't let anything stop them.

Develop a Plan

▶ - Begin by thinking about where you want to go.

- Research it: get a clear picture of the profession or position you want and what it takes to get into it - what qualifications and/or experience? The internet and a good library can help you fill in the details about virtually any field.

▶ - Then ask yourself - how do I get from here to there - from where I am to where I want to be?

- What actions can I take? - taking a course or even enrolling in full- or part-time studies, volunteering or interning for experience, attending seminars, reading books - there are a number of ways you can add to your qualifications.

- How can I approach the field or environment already, even before I've completed any studies or apprenticeships? Don't underestimate the value of networking. Can you volunteer in the field? Can you join an organization or association? In other words, work at something in the field or area already as you prepare yourself for better things. Then, when you're ready for that "big time", you'll already be immersed in that world.

Other Helpful Hints

▶ Get help - enlist your parents, relatives, family friends, teachers - whoever can help you get there. They can help point you in the right direction and help keep your spirits up when things get toughor position you want and what it takes to get into it - what qualifications and/or experience? The internet and a good library can help you fill in the details about virtually any field.

▶ Be realistic - develop a timeline for your goals that's based on research and facts, not wishful thinking. It's important because you don't want to feel discouraged and like you've failed when, in fact, you're just going through the usual growing pains of starting at the bottom.

▶ Reward yourself along the way - celebrate your small successes on the way up, and don't beat yourself up over the small setbacks that are bound to occur. Keeping yourself on a more or less even keel emotionally is the best way to get to where you want, and your support network can help with that. Keep your eye on the ball and try to leave your emotions out of it.

Once you've got a plan and some clear cut goals and steps laid out and you begin to put it all into place, you'll see that everything becomes doable. Don't think about that huge gap between where you are and your end result; break it down into the smaller pieces and steps that will get you from A to B, and there you go, it's an achievable goal.

Work Is the Easy Part...

Those people whom you tend to admire and look up to seem to have everything going for them, from professional success to the tangible rewards of wealth, including dealing effectively with that often bewildering mix of personal and professional pressures that comes along in anyone's life and career.

Acquiring the skills and the background you need for your chosen line of work is one thing, and in a sense, that is the easy part. At the very least, it's an area that where you will be able to find out exactly how you should proceed and where you can go to get answers. Other aspects of finding your way in the world of work and careers will be anything but that straightforward.

The Wild Card

People are always the wild card, and the area where you're most likely to trip and even fall flat on your face. There's no handbook or course you can take that will guide you through your dealings with every type of personality that you'll meet on your way, whether that's in your career or your private life. You can be the salesperson of the year at your branch office and doing fine in every way, and then bang - there's a new sales manager who seems to have made it their personal mission to make sure you don't succeed. It can shake up your plans right down to their foundations.

In the last chapter, I talked about how important it is to learn how to get along with people at work. It's not about finding your next BFF - it's about getting a job done and working towards your goals.

That simple concept of "getting along with others" can take on entirely different dimensions when it goes beyond a simple situation where you don't like someone's style at work or resent your boss' authoritarian air. Sometimes, the implications can be very serious, up to and including results that can be both career and life changing. When the stakes are high, your ability to roll with the punches becomes that much more important.

Every once in a while, though, a situation may come up where you find you have to make a clean break. Sometimes, that is the only solution. How do you know? In some cases, a compromise will keep the peace and let you go on, but in some cases, a compromise is too much. Keep your eye on the "big picture" and ask yourself: Can I compromise and still reach my own goals? Or am I setting aside everything I'm working towards in order to "fit it"? That's really the key question. The breaking point should be where you're giving up your future plans for a temporary solution.

But - don't make a break without having an exit plan in place.

- ▶ Whether it's a work or personal situation, make firm plans about where you will go and what you will do next - there's nothing worse in a time of crisis than being left without a direction.

- ▶ Use your contacts - if it's personal, call your girlfriends, and if it's business, then it's time to look in your contact list to see who can help. You certainly don't have to tough everything out on your own, and it's your support network that will get you through the rougher patches in life no matter where they come from.

Make a decision and move forward

When I left the family business, my brother took the step of launching a lawsuit against me and it got very nasty between us all for a time. I knew in my heart that I'd made the right decision, and that for me the only way to move ahead professionally was on my own. But at the same time, I wanted to have a relationship with my family.

I wanted it all, in other wor ds - and I wanted it on my terms. One memory I have that gets me through bad times, heartache and fear is something my stepdad Bill said to me. I remember I was heartbroken at one particular time and we'd been talking about it for a while when he said to me, "No matter what I say Kirin, the only thing that will get you through is time. Just give it time."

Sure enough, time passed and I learned that no matter how much upheaval occurs and how strongly emotions can run, those emotions begin to soften and fade away. Today, I'm still working on my relationship with the rest of my family, but things are going well.

There is no "master plan" or magic solution to working out major tensions and conflicts. But, I found out there are some things that can help:

▶ **Be patient:** A major rift in a relationship isn't going to heal itself overnight. Bide your time and make little efforts to reconnect. Nowadays, we've got so many ways to communicate, and texting or emailing can be a less intimidating way of staying in touch. Be willing to wait as long as it takes for tempers to calm and the ice to thaw.

- **Be persistent:** Along with patience, you'll have to have the stamina to keep trying in the face of possible rejection or lack of response. It's another aspect of the experience that you'll take with you into the rest of your life. Giving up can't be an option. If one approach doesn't work, you keep at it for a while and give it some time, but then in the face of continued negative response, you come back with another, and then another, as many times as needed.

- **Sublimate the ego:** It sounds like giving up more or less, but it will help you in all areas of your life if you can learn to keep your ego out of the situation - even more so in a serious situation as during a water cooler tiff at the office. What that means is giving up the idea of insisting on who you think was right or wrong along with any feelings you may have about retribution. You may have that burning point you've always wanted to make, the one that proves your case once and for all (in your eyes!) but think about this: what does it change? You can be "right" on your own, or more flexible and tolerant in your approach and maintain good relationships. Let it go - you'll feel better for it I promise! You'll feel like you're only losing a burden to give up that way of thinking. I knew that if I wanted to have my independence along with a good relationship with my family, it meant simply accepting them for who they were and learning to get along.

- **Look for the win/win:** This goes along with the point I've just made above. It doesn't mean having to lose sight of your interests either. Look for ways of reconnecting away from any sources of conflict, and make the occasions work for both parties. You're building a positive basis for your ongoing relationship.

The troubles and the temporary rift with my family came at that very tumultuous time in my life. My Stepfather had just passed away and I was also going through a divorce. Never a dull moment, as they say! But the disruption in my life led me to ask myself a lot of those big questions and the answers I was getting were telling me to go in a different direction.

When you make drastic changes in your life, you have to be prepared for the possibility of drastic consequences - including those you may not have expected.

Giving Up Early Dreams

Every girl has fantasies about the perfect home she'll create as an adult, and I was no different. One of the more heart wrenching parts of the whole separation process was selling the home that we'd lived in. It was my dream home, it really was, the perfect sitcom home and all that. I remember when I first put the offer on the property, the snow was falling - it was an idyllic scene.

It always hurts to give up on something that seemed the answer to a dream. It can even lead you to stay in a situation longer than you should - longer than you know it's working - because you've hitched the memory to a dream. Selling the house felt like ending a chapter in my life. I was closing the door on youthful dreams. It felt strange!

In contrast with the situation that was unfolding with the rest of my family, the split with my husband was going pretty smoothly.

I moved from our leafy neighbourhood and into a condo downtown. My soon-to-be-ex-husband and I had agreed on joint custody of our children, and their presence was the only thing that held me together at first. When they were living in my home, I knew I had to keep things going as normal - buy groceries, clean the floor, do the laundry.

I had to be functional and sticking to the basics really helped.

During the times they were with their father, however, and I was all alone in my new condo, I more or less fell apart. For three or four weeks, I was bedridden. I was in pain.

My kids, while they did keep me going in some ways, were also a source of some of that pain. I didn't want to raise my children in the same kind of broken home that I had experienced as a child.

My relationship with my stepdad was key in the way I turned out as an adult, I know that now. I admired him. He was a blonde haired, blue-eyed former RCMP officer, car salesman and alcoholic in recovery. He had his stories to tell! He married into our Indian family and won us all over. I never once said to him, "You're not my father!" He was a hard kind of personality and I can't say he was affectionate, but he was a huge role model. I even got married in the Bahamas because it was his favourite place! When he got sick, it put everything into perspective

I loved my Stepfather and was influenced by him in many ways, but I still felt the pain of the divorce. My acting out behaviour had nothing to do with our relationship, but the loss of a father is hard on a child, no matter how great any other relationships might turn out to be. It hurt a lot to feel like I was putting my own kids through the same experience.

I know what that did to me. I was an attention seeking child. I was a compulsive liar. I felt, in some strange way, that people wouldn't like me if I "just" told the truth. It wasn't that I would tell a complete untruth, not exactly. I didn't make things up out of nothing, but I did exaggerate and embroider and elaborate on the story until it turned into something else. I felt like, the bigger the story I told, people wouldn't be able to ignore me.

The thing is, it became a habit, completely second nature, and I just continued spinning a web of lies around me until my family decided they'd had enough. They organized a meeting to talk to me about it when I was in my mid-twenties "intervention style". It felt terrible at first, but when I came out and told them everything and admitted to that web of lies, they said, "You know what? We still love you." I realized they weren't going anywhere, and it caused a huge change of heart. I realized I didn't need to tell a big story to attract attention.

They'd been there for me and stood behind me then, and it was part of the reason why I didn't want to let my relationship with them sour permanently later on when things between us took a turn for the worse. I was also keenly aware that I was who I was because of my background and where I'd come from. I couldn't turn my back on it.

An Early Start

I got an early start in the world of work - even before I could legally get paid. I started volunteering at the local hospital when I was 13 years old and I loved it. I loved being around people and helping them at the same time.

My family is made up of very ambitious and aggressive people in terms of getting ahead in the world and in business. When I was a teenager, my mother's attitude was that I was going to work on Friday nights - never mind about going out and getting into trouble! That's when I started working on weekends with my Stepfather at the real estate office.

My family taught me so much by example; it was an education that I couldn't have gotten anywhere else. When I was about 17 years old, my mother and stepdad Bill went to Atlantic City on a holiday. While they were there, my mother noticed people selling these cool shoelaces. They came in different colors and they were selling for peanuts on the famous boardwalk, so she bought several pairs to bring home to me as a gift.

I loved them and gave out some of the pairs to my friends. You know how things are at high school - you wear something new and everyone notices. My friends and I got so many compliments and questions about the shoelaces. People were asking where they could buy them.

I told my mother how popular they were, and she was immediately intrigued by the possibilities. She went back to Atlantic City and bought 10,000 pairs of them. She set up a company to sell them and I went to work 7 days a week in the mall. There was an arrangement at our local shopping malls where you could lease what they called a "cart wheel", being a kind of portable booth. There were several set up in the open areas of the mall in addition to the conventional store fronts. So, I started with one cart wheel in the local mall that I manned for the whole summer. By Christmas I had two more cart wheels in two more shopping malls and I'd sold all 10,000 of those shoelaces. I made something in the neighbourhood of $17,000 that summer and I was thrilled. You either have it or you don't! You're a hustler or you're not a hustler - and I knew I was. That's when I first knew that I was an entrepreneur.

My family had taught me a lot and started me in the direction that I'm still going today. I kept all that in mind when things took a turn for the worse. I go so far as to credit them with giving me the strength to know that I was making the right decisions for me even in the face of their opposition, as strange as that may sound.

We've had our dramas and our ups and downs. I'm working

now with my brother and my mother, but independently, and nowadays, my reward is that the relationships are being rebuilt. Being able to work with my brother at times and with my mom too has been fantastic. My mom has been a real estate agent for more than two decades. She's a very smart and brilliant woman - so I've taken advantage of her expertise.

I've asked my mom to come in to mentor and coach my team at my own brokerage, and she does that once a week. She's an educator and she's a self-made millionaire. No matter where our relationship has gotten to at times, I know that in a way what I'm doing is an extension of my mother's dream, following in her footsteps. She had the same passion for educating people that I do but didn't take it to the same level. That's what I want to add to the family legacy - that's how I want to make my own mark.

Put your pride aside

It always comes back to the same principles, whether you're dealing with personal or professional issues. In my case, it was both! Asking my mother to come and coach my team now was a huge step for me. I really had to swallow my pride. The experience as a whole has taught me a lot.

▶ You can negotiate your way to a "better deal" - you don't have to accept situations as they are, and you don't necessarily have to give away all your ground.

▶ You might be putting your pride aside for now - but pride will come at the end of the process, when you really can have it all. Keep your eye on that end result, and do what you need to in the meantime to get there

Let go of the anger and the fear, and let go of your pride. Know when you need to ask for help. Everything happens for a reason. If you learn from negative experiences in a positive manner, it keeps you going. I learned that life is anything but black and white; it's not about winning and losing, because those are only pinpoints along the way. Life is a series of decisions and the consequences follow from that. In the end, I not only rebuilt my family relationships, but it's working towards my professional goals too!

Asking for help

The same principle applies to business dealings. When you own your own business or work independently, it's easy to isolate yourself, to imagine that you can do it all on your own. Certainly, when you're the boss, there are few people in a position to tell you where you're going wrong. Your employees and associates, in fact, will probably consider it in their own best interests to bolster your ego and focus only on the positives.

When it came to my own business, my real estate brokerage, I didn't want to be that autocratic boss who tells people "do this because I said so!" In addition to my mother's sales coaching, I hired a motivational coach for my team. It cost a lot of money, but I felt it was worth it. I didn't want them to just take my word for everything - I felt they needed to hear it from someone else too.

When I look for new sales agents, one of the first places I turn to is my client list. Who knows the work I do better than someone who is already an investor - someone who invested in my company before they even know me?

It's all about building a team environment. We spend more time in the work environment than our family environment, and I'm very conscious of that fact. People have to want to come to work in order to do their best.

In a brokerage, you're considered self-employed. You're out to fend for yourself. But, I want to build a brokerage that runs like a corporation. I want it to mean more to them than just the physical office where they carry out their work. We have movie nights where we'll all check out a film and then talk about it afterwards - what did you gain from that experience, the film?

I'm never afraid to ask for help - if it will benefit my company and my team, I'm all for it. When you're as humble as you can be, and you stay that humble, asking for other's help when you need it, it clears the path ahead. It's all about the energy that you build together. It's a competitive business, but I want us all to get ahead together - not at each other's expense.

Success Starts In Your Mind

It doesn't matter what you do in life, if your mindset is there, that's half the battle. At the end of the day, it's about keeping your focus no matter what else is going on. That's what got me through my family dramas and the ups and downs of life. I kept my eye on the ball and never let anything take me off my path.

This isn't brain surgery! It's something we all know, but the more you can tell yourself that and keep a positive outlook, the better it works for you. When times are tough, you need to get by just one day at a time. If you can think to yourself that one day I'll wake up and I'll feel better about this, it really does start to come true over time. No matter how bad things get or how a situation can consume you in the moment, you can get over it and keep going.

Persistence and focus

I don't want to sound like those cliché self-help writers. I've read a lot of the books about how to succeed, and they all give you similar messages. But even if you don't identify with a particular writer or situation, they can give you insight on what it means to survive in the world.

Sometimes fear is a good thing - such as being at the point of suicide but you don't go through with it because of fear of the unknown. That's why we experience fear, in fact; ultimately it's to keep us safe. Getting by in the world and making a life that's fulfilling in all aspects is largely a matter of learning to manage fear. When is it a good thing that's keeping you from harm? And when it is something that's keeping you from living the life you want? That applies equally to your personal and professional life.

If you look at anything that you've ever done in your life, whether it's taking a job or not, getting married or not, there's only one thing that will stop you from doing something and it's one four letter word - it's fear.

The ultimate self-help book is very simple - get over the fear and you'll do what you want to do. If you want to leave your job, the only thing that's stopping you from doing it, whatever excuse you want to come up with, it boils down to fear. Fear consumes us.

That's my main lesson: if you can get over the fear, you can do whatever you like. It took me a while to come to my decision to leave both my married life and my family's company as a professional. I spent quite a few nights sweating it out, I'll admit, both before I took any of those drastic steps and afterwards, when I was dealing with the aftermath.

But I learned something very important about fear: it can be a very positive thing in respect to overcoming it. When you overcome your fear and act in your best interests, you feel better about things; in fact you'll feel a huge charge. That's when life gets exciting.

You're always going to have fear in your life. We're emotional creatures. That's how we're programmed. Learning to manage and overcome your fears and emotions is really and truly the key to both happiness and success in your personal and your professional life, I can't stress that enough. It's not that things will automatically get easier; it's that you'll know that you can overcome any difficulties that come along and land on your feet no matter what. That's the real meaning of "success".

Chapter Four

Take a Bold Step

$\mathcal{I}$ve talked about that fateful year when I made so many drastic choices. I think a time like that comes along in everyone's life. It's that moment where you're forced to really look at where you've been, how far you've come, and where you're headed.

Really, that moment could come at any time, but people are creatures of habit, as they say, and we tend to stick with what we know. We'll live in familiar circumstances for as long as it's barely tolerable. It certainly doesn't have to get that dramatic. Like many people, I was living in a situation where a lot of things just weren't working - they weren't super awful, and certainly there are people in the world living under worse circumstances, but I wasn't truly happy, and I wasn't truly fulfilled. I did not feel like I was doing what I was supposed to be doing - I felt held back.

You may get that "trapped in" feeling at any stage of your career, but I think it's especially crucial to consider when you're starting out. Sure, you can expect to start at the bottom of the ladder, and that's true whether your career aspirations lie in the corporate world, in academia or anywhere else. So yes, you can also expect that for a certain amount of time, you'll be paying your dues, working at a job that you may not like or really enjoy. But at the same time, you're taking the opportunities that you'll find to learn all you can about the business you're in and the world in general, and waiting for that break to come your way.

You may decide to take a job that's not so great or even outside your field - we've all got bills to pay, and there's never any shame in earning your keep whichever way you can. But at the same time, you're thinking and planning ahead, and getting yourself ready to take that next step by taking night school courses or volunteering for an indie magazine in your spare time - whatever it takes to get involved in your chosen field and look to the future.

But - and this is a huge but! - there's a big difference between biding your time with a not-so-great job as you learn, prepare and wait for an opportunity and toiling away at a second-rate job indefinitely with no opportunity to get ahead in sight. There's something to be said for the security of a steady pay check, but that can't be all that keeps you where you are. A regular pay check all by itself isn't going to ignite your passions and make you happy.

I think it's particularly important to consider when you're in the beginning stages of your career and life development. The thing is, if you start badly - or don't properly "start" anything at all - you can spend years of your life playing catch up.

When you've just left school, I know that just landing a job - any old job at all - can seem like a Herculean feat. You handed out so many résumés and prepped for so many interviews before you got just this one measly offer! The job market can be very competitive for recent grads, it's no joke. Once you've got that first job and you start paying your own bills, looking for the next job and working on that next opportunity may be the last thing on your mind. It can seem exhausting - You mean I can't just rest here for a while? When I'm done working, the last thing I want to think about is... more work!

Sure you can... you can rest where you are as long as you like, but be careful how long you rest. You don't want to be that person who wakes up one day years down the road to realize they're still toiling away at that second - or third-rate job with nothing at all on the horizon to look forward to. It's that horizon you have to keep in mind - and the longer you leave it empty, the farther away it gets.

Stay True To Yourself

Once you've discovered your passion, you can't let it out of your sight - even if you have to start out somewhere way off your chosen path. Even if it has to be a dream that you're still working towards rather than one that you're living right now, it has to figure in your life some way, somehow, because if you lose it, you'll definitely regret it. Your passion is you - it's what makes you unique.

While it takes a dramatic event for many of us to wake up and re-evaluate our lives and direction, we should all really pause to take stock of things on a regular basis. And, when you can see that something's gotten out of line, and you can honestly tell yourself that you aren't happy and that there's nothing and no way for you to make things right in your current situation, then you have to be strong and take the steps you need to take to make your own future happen.

When I struck out on my own, it was to open up my own company, I was sure about that but let's just say that I was operating on 80% passion and maybe 20% concrete plans in the beginning. I registered my company name in January of 2010, but I honestly didn't know what exactly would come of it. People questioned it. Do you really know what you're doing?? I heard it more than once!

But, there was just something that told me I should do it. When I looked at my life, I knew it was not what I wanted, despite the fact that I had a nice house, drove a nice car, and was married with two kids. I couldn't tell myself honestly that I was truly happy either with my marriage or the way my work was progressing as part of the family business run by my mother and brother. As for my kids, they're the greatest and always have been a vital part of my life since the second they were born. I'm thankful and grateful to them for keeping me centred during all the upheaval.

So there I was, with a company name and not much else. Now, I'm not one to back down from a challenge or take the easy road because I was afraid to try. That doesn't mean, however, that all of it came easy to me. Far from it! I spent many nights tossing and turning, wondering if I'd done the right thing - and with that horrible feeling in the pit of my stomach that I couldn't go back to the way things were even if I wanted to. I'd burned my bridges, at least for the time being.

I'm naturally brash but it's not like I just naturally had the confidence- what I had was the passion, and that's what led me to keep going.

Confidence may not come naturally to you either, but it can be cultivated. You can help to develop confidence within yourself as you work on the passion that will fuel your journey to a fulfilling life.

Start by Taking Stock:

▶ Think about your achievements - no matter how small or how insignificant they may seem, everyone has done something they can be proud of. Whether it was your gold stars in grade school for having your work area cleaned up the quickest week after week, or whether you won medals at the track meet, they're all something to be proud of and that can lead you on to the next point.

▶ Your strengths - your achievements will point to your strengths. For example, cleaning up your work area the quickest points to superlative organizational skills. You can take a mess and make sense of it in no time - that's a valuable skill! If your obvious talents lay more along the lines of track medals, then you may have displayed a competitive spirit and speed, or maybe it was stamina in a long distance marathon -

also very positive qualities.

▶ Your passions - in earlier chapters, we worked on finding your passions. Those are usually also a key to finding your strengths. If your passion lies in helping people, then your strength is surely compassion, for example, and probably also a sense of practicality.

▶ If you're in doubt, ask your family and friends, and those close to you. Sometimes other people see things in us that we don't see ourselves, and they can help point out strengths and accomplishments that you wouldn't have thought of on your own.

Your passions and your strengths will work hand in hand, and your knowledge and pursuit of both of them will help build and sustain your sense of confidence.

Confidence Based in Reality

Remember that confidence is ultimately grounded in reality. You're confident because of your self-knowledge and because you've delved into your deepest dreams and wishes and know them literally by heart. The other way to build on your self-confidence is by preparing yourself for the challenges you know you'll face. You've educated yourself, you've taken courses, volunteered in your field of interest - you've done whatever you can to get ready. All of those things should help to boost your confidence levels.

It's not just about "feeling good" about yourself, or some abstract goal for personal development. Confidence is necessary for success; in fact, by building confidence, you're actually preparing yourself to be successful. Whether you have confidence or doesn't only affect the way you feel, it's a mode and an energy that runs through all of your actions. It affects how you project yourself and how others will perceive you too.

Imagine you go to the doctor for an annual exam and a series of lab and other tests. Your doctor tells you to call back for the test results, and when you do, she says:

Umm... I think this looks pretty much all right. I guess. (insert giggle here) It's a little hard to read but... I think it should be okay. Yah. Sure. It's fine - don't worry about it... You're good.

Would you feel entirely comfortable with what you heard, or would you want to rush out to the nearest lab and get them done again for a second opinion?

Confidence affects your actions and your speech patterns. If your speech is hesitant and sounds unsure, people are less likely to believe you, even if what you're saying is the truth. You have to sound like you yourself believe what you're saying, and for that you need confidence.

Confidence makes you believable - in fact, that's where the term "con man" comes from. It's an abbreviation of "confidence man", meaning a man who's gotten your confidence and trust and then abuses it by stealing your money somehow.

Even during my nights of tossing and turning, there was something that kept me going and moving towards my ultimate goal. Even when I felt like my confidence hit rock bottom as far as opening my own business or trusting in my life changing decisions, I knew I had the skills and the knowledge to do what I wanted to do, and that held me up. I had experience in the real estate business and I was already doing the same kind of work. Despite my doubts, I knew there was nothing rational holding me back. That's how I was able to talk myself into that big, bold step.

I also knew that, no matter how big and bold - not to say drastic! - that next step is, I could achieve it by taking it one step at a time.

▶ Start with the basics - get the ground rules right and the rest can follow. I began with setting up my company legally, getting the logo designed, and finding office space. Every little concrete step, I knew, was taking me just a little farther along the road I'd chosen.

▶ Set realistic goals - it goes hand in hand with starting with the basics. Take things one step at a time and always arm yourself with knowledge about what you're getting into. Keep your end goal as lofty as you like but fill in the middle ground with smaller and achievable goals that will get you and keep you on the right road.

Too much confidence, on the other hand...

There are times when I still lack confidence. I'll admit it, I do have my doubts - every rational human being has them. Doubts are what keep you on your toes, keep you sharp. To be over-confident is not good either, in fact it can be just as harmful and limit your potential as much as not having any confidence at all.

Over-confidence leads to mistakes. You may win a few battles here and there, but you'll lose the war in the end. Aiming too high unrealistically will lead you to miss the very real opportunities that can give you everything you want. Those mistakes will add up, and after a while, a string of them is hard to play down. You can easily end up with a checkered professional record with a lot of career ups and downs that won't look impressive to any future employers and associates.

Know Your Weaknesses

Just as you need to know your strengths, it's important to know the areas where you lack experience, knowledge or ability. Otherwise you won't know what to work on, and how to prepare yourself for your future.

If your sense of self-esteem is delicate or uncertain, this part can be hard. Finding or identifying your weaknesses can be yet another excuse for those little voices in your head to tell you how unworthy you are of success. Don't let yourself turn it into a reason to put yourself down!

Logic and rational thinking can help here too. Your weaknesses and shortcomings aren't a reason to feel badly; you can turn them into stepping stones that will help you move forward towards your goals.

Every "weakness" that you see is just a current situation - and the current situation can always change. What you need is to act. If the issue is a lack of knowledge or skills, then educate yourself. Don't use the excuse "I'm just not good at it!" and leave it the way it is. Math may never be your best subject, and I wouldn't suggest anything involving advanced calculus if numbers have always been the bane of your existence, but a few night school courses in targeted math subjects will do wonders and can at least bring you up to the level of everyday competence.

There are also people known as career coaches or counsellors whose very job it is to help you identify your career priorities and then work on those areas where you aren't as strong as you need to be. Never be afraid to look for the help you need - it's out there.

Knowing your weaknesses doesn't mean dwelling on them.

When you work on them and overcome their effects, it only adds to your confidence. And if confidence is based on self-knowledge, after all, then before you know what you're good at, you also have to know what you're not so great at too.

Let's Get Real

I know what you're thinking - sure, it's easy for you to say now that you've had some success under your belt. All you do is make a list of your accomplishments and voilà - your confidence takes root. What about when you're starting out from nothing, an unknown name in a big world?

Of course I don't mean to say that it's easy or that all that it takes is to make a list or two of the positives and hope for the best. But there's a purpose to every step I'm suggesting. Making that list is helping you to conceptualize and even visualize your strengths. That can't help but be a good start, and serve to point you in the right direction.

If you still have trouble mustering self-confidence, first know that you're certainly not alone. A great many famous people have suffered from lack of confidence and self-esteem at critical times in their lives. It's very much part of the human condition. There are many ways you can help yourself, though, and help to cultivate a sense of confidence that will help you immeasurably throughout your life.

Cultivating Confidence

It can help if you try to see it as a logical process - if you have the strengths and the skills, then why wouldn't you succeed in your chosen field? Like me, you can end up talking yourself into taking the next step just because you can't think of any reasonable or rational reason why not to. It's not the most positive expression of self-determination, but if it works to get you moving in the right direction, then use it!

The negative feelings you may have are the result of emotional conditioning, and that can come about from any number of factors, including things that may have happened in your past, traumatic events, and so on. Boiled down to the essentials, it's about fear, pure and simple. It's those little voices at the back of your head that that tell you not to try because you won't win no matter what you do - you're destined to lose, to fail. Drown them out with a rational point of view and your success will just make sense!

Even in the moments I had of very real despair as my closest relationships unravelled and my work situation also changed so drastically, I knew I had to run with my idea and my dream of owning my own brokerage. I'd found my passion and I had to make it my own - do it my way. That's the strength you'll find too when you find your passion and hold on to it. It's what will sustain you through the bad times when things aren't going well.

Coming from a success oriented family certainly didn't hurt. I'd been raised with the idea that success came from working hard at what you love, and I have to admit it gave me a bit of a competitive edge too. I wanted to succeed to show them I could do it on my own; at the same time our tense relationships caused me even more pain when I realized how much I really owed to my upbringing.

Take Action

Action is always the best solution - the only solution - to overcoming difficulties and resolving those thorny issues in life. Taking a lot of time to think and reflect can seem justified - and I certainly don't look down on anyone who wants to take that route. But sometimes a lot of time spent reflecting turns into a lot of time spent brooding and worrying and overthinking a situation without it making even a smidgeon of difference to how things turn out.

My situation was tense from various viewpoints, but even if it's a much less dramatic case of climbing out of a dead end job, confidence is what leads you to act, and action is its most important result.

In fact, the two elements feed on each other. Action itself can be the best way to kick-start your confidence too.

Act As If

There's a saying or a catchphrase that goes "act as if". For others, it's "fake it till you make it". Either way you want to look at it, the idea is this: imagine your goal. Imagine if you were in the position you'd like to be in, and if you felt the way you want to feel - now try acting as if you were there already. If you want to be a manager or executive, in other words, then try to act as if you were already management material. That means paying attention to the "outside" and it may feel at first as if you're just putting on a show... but what you'll find is that little by little, reality will start to catch up to the façade. If you walk around your office looking and conducting yourself like management material, sooner or later, you'll begin to really believe that you're on a direct path to that goal, and the funny thing is, other people will start to believe it too. Then when that perfect opportunity actually comes up and you're ready to make a grab for it, you'll be walking into a role that seems like it was made for you!

What it does is combine two very powerful tools: visualization and action.

When it comes to cultivating confidence, there are a number of things you can do to help yourself "act as if" you were confident, even before you feel it right down to your bones. As you go through these motions, though, you'll find that these measures can make a difference when it comes to being able to visualize yourself in the role you aspire to. You come to believe that you're capable of getting there and living out your dream, and it will make a difference to everything you do.

The important thing is to act. Act as if and it begins to happen in real life.

Here are some ideas for helping to act as if:

▶ **Dress the part:** No matter what your role is, there's a look that goes along with it. That's not to say that you have to absolutely look like everyone else who works in your office or does your job, and it's not really about fitting in. It's about presenting an image that goes along with your professional role. A "professional" look helps set up your role and lets people know you mean business - no matter what business you're in. It also helps you get into character and strengthen your own belief in your professional persona.

- **Your body language:** Your body language says it all. Stand tall, throw your shoulders back - it really is true that you'll immediately begin to feel the difference. Lift your ribcage and hold your posture through your mid-section. You'll feel like you're "walking taller". Make your strides certain rather than hesitant. Walk confidently and like you know where you're going. Sit up straight, just like Mom always told you. She was right! Good posture is good for your back and your shoulders, and your clothes will hang properly on you too. It has a positive effect on those who see you, especially when it comes to first impressions.

- **Don't be afraid to speak:** Speaking up, asking questions, joining the discussion whether it's at work or on a personal level, all these things will help you reach out and boost your sense of self-esteem. Don't worry about the reaction - people are nicer and more receptive than you think, especially if you begin from a position of having enough interest to ask a question and speak up. These are things that will bring you in contact with other people in such a way that can help you and lead to connections in many different ways. Ask questions, offer an informed opinion, and see where it can lead. Too often we're afraid to speak up - it comes from our time in school, when everyone wanted to sit at the back and sat on their hands when the teacher asked for answers. You're not in grade school anymore! So take part in what's going on rather than sitting back just taking notes. Whenever you take part and reach out, you'll get the energy back and that will feed your confidence and feelings of success.

- **Accentuate the positive:** Take that list of accomplishments and skills and add to it as you go along. Keep it where you can see it often. Take the list of weaknesses (that's supposing you even made a list) and put it in a drawer somewhere - not forgotten, but only to bring it out when you can cross something off that list, and add it to the first one. Remind yourself of the good points often.

- **Don't forget the basics:** All those other things your mother tried to teach you also still hold true too. Get enough sleep, eat properly and get regular exercise. All of those elements will help to boost your mood and make sure that you're operating at your peak.

Taking good care of yourself is part of preparing yourself for life, period - let alone a successful one.

Keep Your Goals In Sight

Even - and especially - if your current circumstances are far from where you ultimately want to be, keep your end goal in sight. Every day, try to do something, act on something that works towards them, no matter how "small" that something is. Every step takes you farther along the way. It will add to your confidence when you can look back and see progress, and you will after a time. It's as if you're starting out on a long road, and you only realize how far you've come by turning around to see how many steps have already been taken.

I actually ended up leasing my office space before I was actually a broker. I didn't have my license yet! People kept telling me that I was putting the cart before the horse and I guess I was - but I just knew it had to come together in the end. I knew if I kept taking steps down that road, the end result would be there when I got that far.

I did end up getting my broker's license not too long after I set up the office. It opened in June of 2011, and outside of having my two children, the whole process has been the most incredible, amazing experience I've ever had.

And actually, when I think about it, getting the office first really did make sense, because from the moment I stepped inside that doorway - even before the decorating makeover I gave it - I felt like I belonged there. It was my place of business. I'd arrived. Getting the broker's license and all that other stuff seemed more like a formality.

When You Really Know

You'll know the same feeling when you get to where you need to be in life. There's an incredible sensation you get when you're doing what you're supposed to be doing - like you fell into just the right groove.

There's a saying that says when you find your true passion, you'll never work a day in your life - because it'll never feel like working at all. That saying is 100% true. You can settle for something safe or that regular pay check over everything else, but you'll never know real satisfaction until you go for your true goal in life. I can promise you that anything and everything you did to get there - all those night courses, all those books you read, all those seminars you went to - will be worth it.

I really feel like I'm coming into my own, and that I know what my path in life really should be. I've never felt so strong in knowing that this is where I am supposed to be, and what I am supposed to be doing.

I ended up here because I took the opportunities put in my path, many of them by reason of my background and family. But, I added one crucial ingredient: I added my own input. Instead of turning out exactly like my mother or step-father, who were admittedly my direct examples and role models in the real estate business, I added my own distinctive spin, and invented my own distinctive role inside it.

Carve Out Your Own Professional Identity

Whether you work on your own, in your own business or as part of a larger company, you'll get the most out of your career if you really make it your own. Put your own stamp on it by making yourself different from the rest.

Think about what you're doing and how you can brand it as your own.

- What can you bring to it? How can you bring your own unique set of strengths, passions and skills to the job in a way that's positive, productive and sets you apart from the rest?

- This way of thinking can by extension also help you identify your best career path. For example, maybe you're a people person with a passion for the medical field - you could certainly open a traditional medical practice, but you could also consider things like community health work or the field of health or medical education.

There are 34,000 plus real estate agents out there in the jurisdiction where I do business. We're becoming a dime a dozen and unfortunately it's led to what I see as a decline in the business environment in general. We're fighting with each other, undercutting each other. That's not what I'm about. Setting myself apart from the rest was not only a personal goal, I felt it was a necessary business goal too.

The immediate and all-consuming goal of most first meetings with a potential real estate client is simple: get the listing. I began to realize that I wasn't even getting to the listings because I always began by asking questions, down to the most basic of issues. Why do you want to sell your house?

The reality is that people often have no idea how much money they really - already! - have, and what they can do with it.

A gentleman came to me wanting to sell his condo. When I asked him the question - why do you want to sell your home? - he told me he'd already bought a new place. According to conventional wisdom, and what seemed to him like common sense, he felt like he had to sell the condo right away before he was left responsible for the bills for two properties.

I went to have a look at his existing condo, and it was absolutely gorgeous. I asked him how much equity he had in the place, (that means how much of it he already owned, as opposed to how much he was still paying off at the bank through his mortgage payments,) and I was surprised to hear that it was a substantial percentage. I did the math, and I was able to show him that he could keep the condo and rent it out while still being able to finance the new property based on the equity he already had. Ipso facto - I showed him how he could actually add to his real estate assets, rather than literally trading one for the other.

Now he has his first income property! I went back to the office and my colleagues asked me, "Did you get the listing?" I told them, "No, I got a rental!"

I showed this man how to buy his first income property, and his excitement was exciting for me in turn. In another case where a couple thought they "had to sell" to get themselves out of deep debt, I was able to show them how to refinance their existing property, pay off 75% of their debts, and how to budget to save their house rather than put it on the market. Instead of getting the listing in that case, I was able to show them how to manage their debts and keep the home they thought they'd have to liquidate to pay them.

Did I make a penny out of it? Not in terms of making a sale. Anything you do in real estate should be a return on your investment - just like in the rest of life. Sometimes, though, that return can come where you don't expect it. I ended up with grateful potential future clients who are mending their finances and I know they'll come back to me when they are ready to invest - and who will be spreading the word about what I've done for them throughout their social circles in the meantime.

Chapter Five

Teaching is Learning and Making it Like a Girl

$\mathcal{T}$eaching is the way I was able to distinguish myself from other real estate professionals in a competitive field, but I recommend it for a number of reasons.

It's a great addition to just about any career. If you can express yourself well, then teaching can add to your professional reputation and help establish your expertise, and of course it has the value of spreading your name farther and wider. Hopefully, the people you educate will tell their friends about you and send more business your way - that's exactly how it's worked out for me. My entire business comes from word of mouth.

When I talk about teaching or education, I'm not only referring to the idea of teaching in a classroom setting, although that's an option too. Community colleges and other institutions often look for professionals to teach evening classes. There are several other options as well, including seminars, workshops, weekend or evening talks and even "webinars" (which, just as it sounds, are seminars given over the internet). It has the potential to fit into pretty much any schedule.

The great thing is that you'll find you will learn as much as you are teaching. The whole process of teaching is really about communication. You have to think about what you do and then try to formulate it in such a way that you'll be able to explain to your students. It makes you analyze what you do and all the various steps and elements that are involved in those everyday tasks you come to take for granted. You'll find it helps in your own understanding of the processes you deal with in turn.

In my case, my "students" are my potential clients. The educational aspect is built right into my business model. But, it can certainly take different forms. If you're a hair stylist, for example, you could give seminars and workshops for potential clients on the latest trends and techniques, and you could also help educate future stylists. If you work in sales, you could teach a weekend course in sales techniques at a community college.

If you're a good writer, then writing is yet another way to expand and add onto an existing career - as I've started to do with this book! You'll go through the same process of having to make sense of what you do and then explain it to someone else. It clarifies theories, procedures and processes in your own mind and you'll find your thoughts evolving as you write - it can actually help you get better at what you do.

Writing also has the effect of spreading your name and your message even farther, as do media appearances. You could be the voice giving out the latest hair styling and make-up tips on a radio show or even a local TV program. All of it feeds back into your primary business with a stream of new clientele.

Now, if you're just starting out, the idea of teaching what you're only just putting into practise yourself may seem far-fetched, but you can always start with the idea of educating your clients or customers about what you do.

That's fundamental to any kind of sales or service industry. The flipside means that you'll be learning as much about your job and industry as you can. And add teaching or educating to your horizon - the one you keep in mind and work towards. It'll be part of your overall strategy of making the most of the opportunities you have.

Make the Most of Your Job

No matter what type of business you're in, there are always ways to get more out of the experience. If nothing else, you should learn something from every job you get - even if it's learning about how you don't want to run a business. Be curious about how things work and why things are done the way they are. You'll begin to understand the principles behind it all.

In my case, the whole process that led me to the educational aspect of my profession that's now so integral and important began with simply wanting to know more about what I did. Sure, I could sell a home and do all the paperwork efficiently, but I wanted more than that. I wanted to find out everything I could. I began by delving below the basic mechanics of buying and selling properties as homes to take a much deeper look at the role of real estate in our economy and how it affects people on an individual level.

What I learned as I progressed in my profession inspired me in turn and sparked the real passion I feel for educating people. There's so much fuzzy information on finances and real estate, in fact the prevailing view is full of faulty logic - so I began to feel strongly that I had to share my practical knowledge of how things really work in the world of finance.

That feeling has grown to the point that I think my main focus is to truly educate people, and if that means I have to hold their hand and go through it all five times before they get it, I have no issues doing so. That's what it will take to change people's minds about the world of finance and their own role in it - and it's a role that everyone needs to grasp for their own sake.

Money Sense

Whether you majored in fine art or business administration, you can't escape the necessity of learning how to deal with money. In my case, it is also part of my vocation - real estate is about finances as much as it is about putting a roof over your head. But, you don't need to become a real estate broker or financial professional yourself to know that the world of money and economics are important to anyone's future.

But I'm just starting out...

I know what you're thinking - wait a second! I just got my first job/first promotion/made my first career move. I can barely manage a decent apartment - I certainly don't have the means or the resources to make investments and there's sooo much time to plan for retirement...

It may be early in your financial life, but it doesn't take much to get started on the right path, however, and what you can do at any point is plan and prepare yourself for your financial future in the same way as you're planning your future career moves.

Protect your credit

This is a big one. I know that once you start making your own money and bringing home your own bacon, the temptation is there to spend it on any number of things. Hey - I've got my massive shoe collection too! I certainly know what it's like. But the debts you accumulate just get bigger and badder and can haunt you later in life when you want to buy a car, let alone a house to live in, an income property or any other kind of asset.

- Make a budget that's realistic. This will really make you think about your money and where you're spending it, and help you prioritize.

- Save up for what you want to buy, but save for your future too. Put money aside for that first down payment along with saving for that great new purse.

- Stick to it! Credit card companies are notorious for offering you more and more credit even as you rack up more and more debt - don't fall into that trap. Make sure you don't let your love of shoes ruin your future credit rating. Tell your credit card company in writing that you don't want credit increases above a certain limit that you know you can handle - that means paying it off in full, not over a 20 year payment schedule!

The time to think about finances is while you're young. It's especially important among people 20 to 40 years old because they're the generation who is going to be stuck living in debt if something doesn't change.

I know - you want to party! There's nothing wrong with having a good time now and then, and I certainly don't want to make it seem like you have to give up everything you enjoy to build for your future, but make the future your priority and party when you can - not the other way around. That's the difference. When you're young, nobody looks 20 years ahead, but ironically that's exactly when you can make the biggest difference to your future. It's much, much harder to try and repair your finances and get started when you're in your late 30's or 40's and gets harder still, if it's even possible, after that.

Time goes by so quickly - don't let it slip by with bad financial habits.

Life Is Not Just About Money And Work

There used to be a TV commercial where a man was promoting his hair replacement system, and the tag line was "I'm not just the president of the company, I'm also a client". When it comes to self-help books, I'd probably put that the other way around - I've read tons of them, and I write a little too.

The principles we all talk about in terms of trying to help people often boil down to the same ideas -albeit with variations in method and specific applications.

Napoleon Hill was one of the very first writers in the area of personal development or so-called self-help books. He wrote his most famous work, Think and Grow Rich in 1937 and it's still one of the best-selling books of all time, selling millions and millions of copies because what he says works. He believed that success begins in the mind, with your attitudes and beliefs. What's inside of you is what will come out of you, in other words. Those old school principles are still true - it's about how you apply the information.

I know I'm a believer. I love all the great self-help teachers, like Bob Proctor. I love Anthony Robbins. I remember reading his book Awakening the Giant and thinking: we all know this! It's built on a solid understanding that goes back to psychology and early childhood development. We're all born with the potential to succeed but it becomes dampened by what we learn in childhood during the process of socialization and institutionalization. It tends to squash that creative, entrepreneurial spirit that's inside all of us and turns us into people who follow rather than lead, and who accept a lesser role in the world without questioning it. All you need to reignite your inner potential is a change in attitude - that's what all self-help books boil down to at their most basic essence. Everything I talk about in terms of starting your career and making your way in the world is focused first on attitudes and ideas, and then on putting them into action - and never on settling for anything less than what you want out of life. Even in my own particular application of real estate, the principles are the same: think for yourself and then take action.

Sometimes it does take another voice to reiterate something we already known in our hearts and souls.

If you're persistent and stick to the basic principles, it will work. You've got to believe in the power of the universe, to build and act on your passions and believe that what you put out will come back to you in return.

But that doesn't mean that it ever really gets easier, no matter how much success you rack up, or how many achievements you can point to.

It's Never Over... Stamina is Your Strength

I remember when I finished school and first got my real estate license, bought my first condo and moved into it - living on my own for the first time. For so long, those had been my dreams and stated goals. Sure, I was always looking down the road at where I could possibly progress to later in my career, but the next step on the road seemed far off in the distance, and I guess I had the idea that I'd get to a certain place in my life and I'd be there. I'd arrive. I'd be at some kind of plateau where I could settle in for the long haul and things would be... easier.

Most of us think that way. You hold a dream as you're growing up, a vision of what you think your life will be like - maybe it's a TV-style fantasy with a cool loft apartment in an exciting city with a fabulous and glamorous job, a closetful of great clothes and a social life full of friends and fun. If I get there, you're thinking, I'll have made it.

But guess what happens? When you move into that apartment - and it's likely to be a lot smaller than you thought on your starting salary - it comes with a stack of bills to pay, including a hefty credit card bill from all those clothes you just bought! And your career takes up a lot more time than you thought, especially if you have any hope of being able to advance. Your weekends and other time off seem so short and you have a million things to do from shopping to laundry. Just keeping food in the fridge and eating regularly and well takes time and effort when you're on your own, and a whole new layer of responsibility once a relationship and children come into the picture. There is no plateau. You never really "arrive" anywhere except at the beginning of another stage, another step. There's always more effort to make.

Even as I've been writing this book there have been ups and downs in my life, many obstacles and those little everyday successes that keep me going. Even though I love owning my own business, I'm constantly reminded that I too am still being tested every day with all the inherent challenges, the trials and tribulations of finances, payroll, up-keep and being the person that's driving all the sales. It's a lot to take on. It's hard work that never lets up.

It's my passion and drive that keep me going. That's why it's so important to find your true passion and pursue it from the beginning - passion is what will sustain you as you go along. It's the fire that keeps burning even in those moments when you feel tired and you may be tempted to let up the fight.

Having More Than a Career

Although my focus in this book has largely been on career building and the world of work, I've also mentioned family matters and relationships. Naturally, for a balanced life, you need more than a career or job and your passions will extend to your personal relationships and family life too. You want it all - just as I do! - but I'll warn you that it becomes that much harder. Your personal life needs just as much time and attention as your workday life.

The word "balance" is a good one to use here, because it does feel like a constant balancing act. There will be times when you'll find you have tough choices to make, and when children come into the picture, I can tell you from personal experience that while your priorities may become clearer, the decisions never do. In fact, the stakes get higher and the decisions more crucial.

The difficulties of maintaining some kind of balance are tough on women, there's no denying it, and they've done the research to prove it too. The Center for Talent Innovation (www.worklifepolicy.org) is a non-profit think tank based in New York City. They specialize in developing research and projects around diversity and talent management, including the Task Force for Talent Innovation, a private sector group comprised of 71 companies operating in 190 countries across the world that looks to help corporations best use the human resource talent available across issues of gender, generation and culture. Their research suggests that 41% of women who reach executive status in their careers have no life partners or significant romantic relationships and that 40% of them don't have children. Those are sobering figures.

It's a reality - marriage and children can derail your best laid career plans in ways that they just don't for your male counterparts at work, no matter what their relationship status is. Men don't seem to have to make the choice between giving career or family their principle focus, whereas women often feel they will (and do!) shoulder the burdens of both.

Maybe for you, it's your career that's derailing your plans for a family and home life. Your home is your clear focus, but in today's world, you know you have to work as well, and if you don't pay any attention to job or career matters at all, you'll be stuck in a low level position with no prospects of working your way up. You end up with a great family and a series of boring, unfulfilling jobs that are wasting your natural talents because you don't have the skills or experience to move on. What's worse is that the sense of dissatisfaction and lack of recognition of your talents and skills can cross over into your family life and lead to a general sense of frustration and even depression that your spouse and children will feel too in various ways.

Whether that "balance" is shifted in favour of one or the other, for most women, juggling career and family will always be an issue. We really do need to look after ourselves as whole people, including all facets of our lives.

There's no magic solution to figuring all of it out, but there are some ways that can help you to manage it better.

▶ Decide on your priorities - what is number 1? If I'm on the verge of closing a big real estate transaction and I get a phone call telling me my son's been in an accident and is in the hospital, my priorities are crystal clear. Potentially losing a deal to bad timing might be wrenching from a business perspective but when you know what your first priority is at all times, it does make some of the decisions clearer.

▶ Schedule time for personal life the way you schedule it for business appointments. Personal relationships will falter from lack of attention whether it's about boyfriends, life partners, children or good friends.

▶ Schedule time for just you, making time to unwind

112

or pursue new interests, make new friends, or just to take stock and measure, every once in a while, whether all the parts of your life are where you want them to be, and if not, how you can get there. When you're juggling a lot of balls in the air at any given time, life can be so busy you don't realize that a situation's getting out of control, or your time is being gobbled up by something that you should really be relegating to the back burner.

▸ Never forget the basics. Always make sure you eat right and get enough sleep and exercise. When you have small children, you see right away that their mood is affected by things like hunger. A hungry baby is cranky and a hungry child can't concentrate on schoolwork. The same is true of us as adults - don't forget to look after yourself because it's the bedrock of everything you do in life. You owe it to yourself to give yourself the strength to tackle everything that's on your plate.

You may find yourself making some hard decisions at any given time, like giving up on a hobby you really love because you can't find the time anymore. Remember, though, that nothing is permanent and conditions change over time. If you can't pursue a beloved pursuit at the moment, then plan ahead for a time that you can. Keep it on your horizon and in your concrete plans for the future, and then you can work to make those more favourable conditions happen too.

In my case, I'm fortunate enough to be able to get some help - I've hired a nanny. She's an invaluable part of my life now, giving me the extra time to devote on my business while knowing that my children's needs are being more than just adequately met.

Finding a little extra help may be a possibility for you too, even if you're single and making your way on a starting salary. It doesn't have to cost a lot. If housework is the one area that is really suffering, then maybe a once-a-month visit from a professional maid service is what you need to give you that little bit of extra time and a cleaner apartment too. Many Laundromats offer a "wash and fold" service that will do your laundry for a set fee. Occasional babysitting, grocery delivery, personal shoppers - sure, these services do all cost a bit of money, but even if you can't afford them all the time, used once in a while they can take some of the burden off your shoulders and give you a bit of a boost too.

Balance will come to your life because you work at it constantly. It won't happen by accident, and it's never a fixed state. It's something that fluctuates all the time and the sooner you start to keep it in mind, the better off you'll be.

Success is Being On the Road

Think about your future - it's never too early to start. Getting into good habits when it comes to your finances, your credit and how you allocate your time and energy early in life makes it that much easier to maintain later on. It's definitely harder and sometimes even impossible to break bad habits and reconstruct finances or ruined relationships after the fact than it is to maintain hood practices.

Find yourself, find your passion and make it part of your whole life, not just something you think about once in a while. Think about what you can offer, stay focused and then get it out there to the world.

I know I don't consider myself "financially successful" as yet. I've got a long way to go according to my measuring stick, but I'm here working on it every single day. The mere fact that I've passed my first anniversary of being in business while raising two children (even if I have a nanny!) - I feel like a success just by pulling through even though I know I'm still growing and learning all the time.

Take the time to savour where you are and everything you've achieved so far. Success means being on the road to your future - no matter at what point you're at right now.

I'm excited to be on this part of my journey through life

115

and I as learn, I'll write about it and share my hard earned knowledge with you, my readers present and future.

I can hardly wait for the next step - can you?